Biographies of Early Century Black Americans

Historical Black Figures

(1700s – 1800s)

Y
N ME

Copyright

Dedication

I dedicate this book to my remarkable dearly departed mother, Catherine Harper May, who was a trailblazer and inspiration to those who knew her.

Contents

Acknowledgments

I sincerely thank Dr. Ruth Tappin whose insightful suggestions and guidance made this book possible. I extend my gratitude, also, to Mrs. Sandra Dodge for her editorial skills and general assurances. Special thanks to Louise Minks who so generously granted me permission to use her artistic rendition of Lucy Terry Prince, one of the most remarkable characters in this book.

Preface

"There's no place like home!"

For African Americans, that warm, familiar sentiment can seem paradoxical—an absurdity, almost. After being captured in tribal wars or stolen through raids on their villages by other Africans, millions of African men, women, and children were then sold or traded to White European profiteers, to be sold as property in the New World. Forcibly taken from their homeland, enslaved, and now planted in the New World, these unfortunate souls and their descendants labored under the lash for centuries.

Divested of family, language, customs, and traditions, these enslaved Africans were stripped of virtually every vestige of human dignity. Not one of the most basic and elemental God-given human rights enjoyed by even the poorest White, and taken for granted by their captors, was theirs.

Although the Black American has been integral in the establishment, development, and continued growth of America, to their White owners these Africans and their descendants were mere property, subject to their owner's whim and will. To the White Europeans who settled in America, this land was *their* land; to them, the forcibly settled Black men and women—and their descendants—could never be American; this land could never be theirs, and America could never be their home sweet home.

The purpose of this book is to share highlights of what is known about 31 interesting Black men and women from the 18th and 19th centuries. The men and women listed here are but a fraction of the vast numbers of Black persons who rose above their bondage and circumstances and, along with their White brethren of good conscience, made this country great. Their presence in America, and their great love for this country, proclaims, "*There is no place like home. We are Americans and this is our home, too.*"

This book was purposely designed to present succinct bios of 31 noteworthy historical Black men and women. It can be a valuable teaching tool in schools, and a different character may be studied for each day of Black History Month. In 2022, Black History Month spans Tuesday, February1 – Tuesday, March 1. It is my hope that readers will be inspired and motivated to explore more deeply the history of the African American experience in America.

Miriam Y. McCarthy, B.S.

Foreword

Spanning the 18th and mid-19th centuries (1700-1870), this book provides a tantalizing glimpse into the lives of 31 Black men and women born in the early colonial, antebellum, and post Civil War periods of American history. They lived at a time when the terms "Black American" or "African American" did not exist in the lexicon, for, as decided by the 1857 Dred Scott *v* Sanford Supreme Court case, people of African descent were not considered to be Americans; that right would not be bestowed upon them until 1868.

Yet, homeless, or stateless, though reduced to the status of property and denied the constitutional rights afforded their White brethren, Black men and women labored to make America a great nation. As this book shows, somehow, against impossible odds or perhaps just the sheer luck of having owners of good conscience, some Blacks managed to gain their freedom and rise above the social and economic constraints that consigned them to another type of enslavement: that of the mind and intellect.

The reader may be familiar with some of the illustrious characters represented in this book, such as Sojourner Truth (1797-1883) or Scott Joplin (1867-1917). However, it will surely be enlightening to learn of less familiar individuals such as the intrepid Lucy Terry Prince (1730-1821) who fought and won a land-right case before the nascent Supreme Court, or the talented and much-admired Dr. James Derham (1762-1802), who was the first Black unlicensed practicing physician that treated the sick—regardless of color. This book can make a useful contribution to school curricula and, because it focuses purposefully on 31 characters, it can be used as an aid in teaching Black History during Black History month.

R. M. Tappin, Ph.D

Introduction

This book is not a comprehensive account of the intrepid Black men and women who rose above their circumstances to leave their "footprints in the sands of time"[1]. Rather, it is a concise account of 31 unique and talented Black individuals who, though confronted by seemingly insurmountable religious, social, and economic barriers, broke through the chains of slavery and racism that sought to subjugate them in every way imaginable.

Individuals who contributed something unique to their times—from early colonial days through the Reconstruction period after the Civil War, are highlighted in this book. Some were born into slavery and experienced life as a slave, then became free men and women. They might have gained freedom through manumission, purchasing their liberty, running away, or, eventually, by the Emancipation Declaration of January 1, 1863, after the Civil War ended.

To fully appreciate the accomplishments of these men and women represented in this book, the reader should keep in mind the reality of the era in which the individuals in this book lived.

---

[1] http://www.potw.org/archive/potw232.html

The book is suitable reading in middle school, high school, and college. Parents and/or teachers can use it to teach children about a new character for each day of Black History Month. Parents and teachers are encouraged to do further research on the Black men and women who helped build this country though their free and forced labor during slavery, through their intellectual accomplishments, and through service in defense of this country.

LUCY TERRY PRINCE

[1730-1821]

First Known Black American Author

Conceptualization of Lucy Terry Prince by artist Louise Minks

c. 1724[1]: Lucy Terry[2] (married name "Prince") was born in West Africa and stolen by slave traders when she was around five years old. She arrived on the shores of New England in the state of Rhode Island, a slave port at the time.

c. 1730: She was sold to the Ebenezer Wells family of Deerfield, Massachusetts. The Wells were childless and as a result treated their slaves as "servants for life"[3]. The implication of such a benevolent attitude was a kind nurturing environment. Given the

---

[1] Conflicting reports state Lucy Terry's date of birth.
[2] Lucy Terry was also known as Luce, Bijah's Luce, or Luce Abijah
[3] www.massmoments.org

fact that Lucy was literate and wrote poetry, the Wells must have allowed their servants to read and write. It is worth noting that this situation was totally contrary to slave treatment and is a reflection of the hearts and minds of one individual family out of hundreds.

1746: Lucy witnessed the Abenaki Indian raid on the village of Deerfield, Massachusetts; she was 22 years old at the time[4] and wrote a poem called *Bars Fight*[5], memorializing the event and identifying those who perished in the raid. The poem was preserved orally for over 100 years after the event, and published in 1855; it is her only surviving work. It is also the earliest surviving literary work by an enslaved Black person in America.

1749: The colonies were being swept up in what was called the Great Awakening. A spiritual movement was drawing slaves and Whites into Christianity. Lucy was very affected by the movement and, at the age of 25[6], she was baptized. Previously, as a child in 1735, she had been baptized while enslaved.

1756: Abijah "Bijah" Prince (1706-1794) was a free Black man in Deerfield. Though twenty years Lucy's senior, Bijah

---

[4] Online reports of Lucy's age at the time of the massacre range from 15 or 16 to 22 years old. In the very first line of the poem, Lucy reported the date of the Bars Fight as August 25, 1746. If she were 15 or 16 at the time of the fight, then Lucy would have been born six or seven years later than most reports. It would seem that she was actually around 22 years old when the attack occurred, and that she wrote the poem while it was still fresh and raw in her memory.

[5] "Bars" is an old English term for meadows.

[6] Reports of her age at the time of her baptism as an adult range from 19 to 22 years old.

proposed to her and Lucy accepted. On May 17, 1756, Lucy became Lucy Terry Prince. Though enslaved at the time of her wedding, sometime later Lucy gained her freedom either through manumission by the Wells[7], or through purchase by Abijah[8].

The Prince family began their married lives living on land owned by the Wells. In this setting Lucy's talent and popularity as a speaker and poet emerged. Lucy was an engaging storyteller and poet, and her reputation as an eloquent and witty speaker developed and spread.

c. 1760s: Colonel David Field of Deerfield granted Bijah 100 acres of land in Guilford, Vermont (VT). Bijah, Lucy, and the rest of the family moved to Guilford for a short period of time, but eventually moved back to Deerfield, and then to Sunderland, VT, where he was an original grantee of 300 acres of land. Bijah was the only grantee to actually homestead on the land, working on the property by himself.

1764: Colonel Eli Bronson contested Bijah's ownership of the land and acquired one-half of the Prince family's land; the family sued. The case went up to the newly-instituted United States Supreme Court; Samuel Chase was the presiding judge. Even though the Prince family engaged a lawyer, Isaac Tichenor[9], Lucy argued the case herself and won the lawsuit. Other reports

---

[7]http://americancenturies.mass.edu/classroom/curriculum_12th/unit1/lesson9/lucy_terry.html
[8]https://www.britannica.com/biography/Lucy-Terry
[9]Isaac Tichenor went on to become governor of Vermont in 1797

refute Lucy going before the federal Supreme Court and assert the case was heard in the Circuit Court of Bennington, VT, with Associate Judge Samuel Chase of Maryland presiding. Whichever is true, the sustained fact is that Lucy Terry Prince presented her case before the court and won. Reportedly, the presiding Judge declared Lucy had made a better argument than he had ever heard from a lawyer in Vermont[10].

1780: The Prince family came under attack when an affluent and politically influential White man, John Noyce, and his wife, Ormas, whose property abutted that of the Prince family, sought to usurp the Prince family's rights and steal their property. The land dispute continued for several years and Lucy Prince eventually appealed successfully to the Governor and the Council of the State of Vermont for help.

1785: At a meeting attended by Governor Thomas Crittenden and other officials in Norwich on June 7, Lucy Prince's appeal was upheld. The Noyces were found to have oppressed and caused Lucy and her husband injury[11,12].

1794: Abijah Prince passed away.

---

[10]Proper, David R. (1992) "Lucy Terry Prince: "Singer of History"," Contributions in Black Studies: Vol. 9 , Article 15. Available at: https://scholarworks.umass.edu/cibs/vol9/iss1/15

[11]http://americancenturies.mass.edu/classroom/curriculum_12th/unit1/lesson9/lucy_terry.html

[12]These land disputes helped to impoverish the Prince family.

1803: Lucy moved to Sunderland, Vermont. Every year, until her death she rode over one hundred eighty miles on horseback between Guilford and Sunderland to visit her husband's grave.

1821: Lucy Terry Prince passed way July11 at 97 years of age in Sunderland, Vermont. Reverend Lemuel Haynes, the first Black minister ordained in the Congregational Church in the United States, delivered her eulogy. He stated "Tyrants and oppressors sink beneath Terry's feet". He was alluding to her poetry and her oratory. Obituaries at that time were traditionally very short, and there were no public notices of deaths among Black folks. Lucy's obituary was printed in the Vermont Gazette and the Greenfield, Massachusetts newspaper recognized her as very memorable. Where she is buried is not known.

1855: *Bars Fight* was published by Josiah G. Holland in *The History of Western Massachusetts*[13].

[***NOTE:*** Apart from the battles over land rights, there were other issues of denial of rights addressed by Lucy; for example, one of their sons was denied admission to Williams College, Williamstown, Massachusetts, because of his race. Lucy argued before the college's Board of Trustees for three hours using scriptures to plead her son's case for admission to the school. The Board of Trustees did not change their position. It has been

---

[13]http://americancenturies.mass.edu/collection/itempage.jsp?itemid=7779&level=advanced&transcription=1&img=

reported that the many legal battles that Bijah and Lucy fought impoverished the family.]

Lucy Terry Prince's poem is considered the oldest known literary work by an African American. The 18th-century spelling and commonly used words are retained in the poem.

Bars Fight[14]
by Lucy Terry Prince

August, twas the twenty-fifth,
Seventeen houndred forty-six,
The Indians did in ambush lay,
Some very valiant men to slay
Twas nigh unto Sam Dickinson's mill,
The Indians there five men did kill.
The names of whom I'll not leave out,
Samuel Allen like a hero foute,
And though he was so brave and bold,
His face no more shall we behold.
Eleazer Hawks was killed outright,
Before he had time to fight,
Before he did the Indians see,
Was shot and killed immediately.
Oliver Amsden he was slain,
Which caused his friends much grief pain.
Simeon Amsden they found dead

[14]https://allpoetry.com/Bars-Fight

Not many rods from Oliver's head.

Adonijah Gillett, we do hear,

Did lose his life which was so dear.

John Sadler fled across the water,

And thus escaped the dreadful slaughter.

Eunice Allen see the Indians comeing

And hoped to save herself by running:

And had not her petticoats stopt her,

The awful creatures had not cotched her,

Not tommyhawked her on the head,

And left her on the ground for dead.

Young Samuel Allen, Oh! lack-a-day!

Was taken and carried to Canada.

BARZILLAI LEW
[1743 – 1822]

Professional Musician and Soldier

Barzillai Lew
Source: Public Domain

1743: Barzillai Lew was born free on November 5 in Groton, Massachusetts, to free Blacks, Primus and Margaret Lew[15].

1760: A gifted musician, for 38 weeks he was a fifer under Capt. Farrington[16] on the side of the British during the French and Indian War, which lasted from 1754 to1763.

---

[15]https://libguides.uml.edu/c.php?g=1125577&p=8214995

c. 1766: Lew purchased the freedom of Dinah Bowman (1744-1837) for $400[17]. The very light-skinned Dinah was owned by Major Abraham Blood; subsequently, Lew married Dinah and between them had 13 children.

1775: Because of his musical excellence, Lew was asked to join the colonists' War for American Independence. He agreed and was a fifer in the 25th Regiment of Massachusetts, stationed at Cambridge, under Capt. John Ford. He was on the field at Bunker Hill, a major battle in the revolution. His playing on the fife and the drum helped encourage the soldiers.

1776: Lew was selected to play the fife in the Battle of Ticonderoga (July – December, 1776)[18]; this resulted in another victory for American independence.

After the war, Barzillai bought land and became a farmer and a cooper. It turns out that his entire family was musically gifted. They played before audiences from Portland, ME, to Boston, MA.

1822: Barzillai Lew passed away, aged 79, and was buried in Claypit Cemetery, which was part of Dracut, Massachusetts, at the time. The cemetery was also known as "the Old Burying Ground". Today, that area is known as "Pawtucketville". As of

---

[16]https://www.nps.gov/people/barzillai-lew.htm
[17]According to www.inflationdata.org, $400 in 1766 is worth approximately $14,368 in 2021 (https://www.officialdata.org/us/inflation/1766?amount=400)
[18]https://primaryresearch.org/barzillai-lews-revolutionary-war-pension-file/

2019, no headstone marked Lew's grave; however, there are plans to erect a marker at the cemetery in his memory.

[***NOTE:*** Dinah Lew passed away 15 years after her husband's death. Records in the 1818-1872 United States Revolutionary War Pension Payment Ledgers showed that she received a pension based on her deceased spouse's military service as a fifer[19]. At a time when most Black people were enslaved and considered to be property and less than full human beings in America, the Lew family was highly regarded, highly educated, property owners, and considered to be the most gifted musicians of their time.]

[19]"United States Revolutionary War Pension Payment Ledgers, 1818-1872," database with images, *FamilySearch* (https://familysearch.org/ark:/61903/1:1:Q24Q-K61J : accessed 28 November 2021), Barzillia Lew in entry for Dinah Lew, 04 Mar 1831; citing Massachusetts, United States, NARA microfilm publication T718 (Washington D.C.: National Archives and Records Administration, 1962), roll 16; FHL microfilm 1,319,396.

PRINCE DEMAH BARNES
[1745 – 1778]

Portrait Artist

Portrait of William Duguid (1773) by Prince D. Barnes
Source: Public Domain

1745: Very little information exists about Prince Demah Barnes[20]; however, he was born into enslavement and raised in Marlborough, Massachusetts (MA). His mother, Daphney, was enslaved to prominent businessman Henry Barnes and his wife Christian Barnes. Prince and Daphney were baptized at Trinity Church, Boston, MA, in the year of his birth.

---

[20]https://www.themagazineantiques.com/article/prince-demah-barnes-1/

1769 (?): Christian Barnes noted Demah Prince's talent as a painter. Mrs. Barnes wrote to a friend that her husband had bought Demah. The stated purpose for the purchase was to improve Demah's genius in painting. In a letter to a friend, Christian Barnes referred to Demah as "our Limner[21]" and opined that he was more talented than the famous portrait painter, John Singleton Copley[22].

1770: Barnes took Demah to London to receive formal training in the art of portrait painting. According to Christian Barnes, in a letter to Elizabeth Murray Smith, Mr. Barnes hoped to benefit from Prince's developed talent.

1771: In correspondence with his wife in February, Barnes reported Prince was receiving lessons from British Portrait Artist Robert E. Pine. There is speculation that Pine's father was of mixed ancestry, and Pine most likely influenced Demah politically and artistically. In a letter to Elizabeth Murray Smith, Mr. Barnes stated that he did not allow Demah to associate with "any of his own colour here"[23], fearing their political influence upon him. Prince returned to America in July 1771. Eventually, Pine, too, came to America.

1773: Prince painted a portrait of a Scottish merchant, William Duguid, which he signed; it survives today. Between January

---

[21]A limner is a painter of miniature portraits
[22]John Singleton Copley was the most notable portrait painter of the Boston elite during colonial times.
[23] https://www.themagazineantiques.com/article/prince-demah-barnes-1/

and November of 1773, at least nine advertisements appeared in the *Boston Newsletter*, promoting Prince's services as a portraitist and describing him as a genius at this art. One advertisement in the *Massachusetts Gazette: and the Boston Weekly Newsletter, February 4, 1773*, under the heading "**At Mr. M'Lean's, Watch-Maker**..." declared, "He takes faces at the lowest rates"[24].

1775: Prince's owners, the Barnes family, were British Loyalists. Forced to hastily return to England due to the growing unrest in the colonies, they abandoned their entire estate in Marlborough, MA, including Prince and his mother. After Barnes and his wife returned to England, Prince considered himself a free man; however, no legal papers exist attesting to Prince's freedom from his enslavement. Subsequently, Prince dropped the surname "Barnes" and identified himself and his profession as "Prince Demah, Limner."

1777: During the American Revolution, Prince enlisted in the militia as a free man, under the name of "Prince Demah"[25]; his length of service in the Massachusetts Bay militia extended from 1777 to 1778.

---

[24] https://www.masshist.org/dorr/volume/4/sequence/309

[25] "Massachusetts, Revolutionary War, Index Cards to Muster Rolls, 1775-1783," database with images, *FamilySearch* (https://familysearch.org/ark:/61903/1:1:Q2RW-Y4WG : 17 March 2018), Prince Demah, 30 Apr 1777; citing Military Service, Massachusetts Bay, British Colonial America, Massachusetts State Archives, Boston; FHL microfilm 2,021,709.

1778: Prince became gravely ill—perhaps from smallpox, which was endemic at the time. After writing his will, in which he left everything to his mother, Prince Demah died. A record of his death exists at Trinity Church, Boston, which is the place of his burial.

[***NOTE:*** Although very little information about Prince Demah survives, he is the only known enslaved artist whose paintings are in still existence today.]

PHILLIS WHEATLEY
[1753 – 1784]

The First Slave of African Descent and only the Third Woman to have published a Book

Phillis Wheatley.
Source: Public Domain

1753(?): Wheatley was born in the Senegambia region of West Africa[26]—possibly in modern-day Gambia or Senegal.

1761: She was stolen from Africa, brought to Boston in July, and purchased by the Wheatleys to be a house servant. She was frail, with poor health, throughout her life. The Wheatleys named her

[26] https://www.loc.gov/item/today-in-history/september-01/

after the ship, "*The Phillis*", on which she was transported and she assumed her owner's name after she was baptized.

1762 -1763: Mrs. Susanna Wheatley and her daughter, Mary, taught Phillis to read. She was a very fast learner and, though she did not speak or write the English language before her captivity, within 18 months of her arrival in America she was reading the Bible. Recognizing her intelligence, the Wheatleys educated her in the humanities. Wheatley quickly mastered Greek, Latin, and English Literature.

While serving the Wheatleys and their guests, Hussey and Coffin, Phillis overheard the guests recount their harrowing escape from a storm at sea, and wrote the poem *On Messrs Hussey and Coffin*[27]

1767: On December 21, at the age of 14, Phillis published her first poem, *On Messrs Hussey and Coffin*, in the Newport Mercury. In that year, she also wrote *An Address to the Deist*[28] and *An Address to the Atheist*[29]. Two years later, she wrote *Atheism,* which was similar in message and tone to *An Address to the Atheist.*

1768: Wheatley wrote *To the King's Most Excellent Majesty*[30], a tribute to King George on the occasion of the repeal of the Stamp Act Law.

---

[27] http://www.phillis-wheatley.org/on-messrs-hussey-and-coffin/
[28] http://www.phillis-wheatley.org/an-address-to-the-deist/
[29] http://www.phillis-wheatley.org/an-address-to-the-atheist/

1770: In tribute to a popular preacher upon his death, Wheatley wrote *An Elegiac Poem on the Death of that celebrated Divine, and eminent Servant of Jesus Christ, the Reverend and Learned Mr. George Whitefield.* Mr. Whitefield was Selina Hasting's chaplain; Hastings, the Countess of Huntingdon, would soon become Wheatley's patron. Wheatley gained recognition for her poetry after penning the elegy.

1772: Phillis Wheatley's authorship of her poetry was challenged in court; however, 17 Bostonians—including John Hancock—attested in writing to her authorship, and she prevailed against the scurrilous accusations.

1773: The Wheatleys traveled to London where Selina Hastings funded publication of Phillis's first book of poems entitled *Poems on Various Subjects, Religious and Moral*, which was published on September 1, 1773; at the time, Wheatley was only the third woman to have published a book[31]. Her poetry was successful and popular, enabling her to purchase her freedom.

1774: Mrs. Susanna Wheatley died in 1774.

1775 - 1776: After Wheatley wrote a tribute to George Washington in 1775, Washington invited Wheatley to read the poem to him at his home in 1776. The title of the poem was *To His Excellency, George Washington.*

---

[30] https://bit.ly/39NpXNs

[31] http://www.phillis-wheatley.org/facts/

1778: Mr. Wheatley died in 1778. Most of the Wheatley family passed on, leaving Phillis no support or funding source. White publishers were still refusing to publish her work. Wheatley married a free Black, John Peters, with whom she had three children. All of her children died in infancy. Wheatley fell on hard times. She worked in a boardinghouse to support herself. Wheatley continued writing on a variety of subjects, still without a publisher. "*On Being Brought To America from Africa*" was her best known work.

1784: Wheatley wrote what was possibly her last poem, *An Elegy, Sacred to the Memory of the Great Divine, the Reverend and the Learned Dr. Samuel Cooper*[32] (1725-1783), shortly before her death. Dr. Cooper was one of the 17 men who attested that Phillis was the author of her poetry.

On December 5, 1784, at the age of 31, Phillis Wheatley died of pneumonia during childbirth at a boarding house, alone and impoverished; her newborn daughter passed away on the same day. Wheatley was buried at Copp's Hill Burying Ground Boston, Suffolk County, MA.

[32] https://bit.ly/3ojdhGL

PAUL CUFFEE

[1759-1817]

Quaker Businessman, Commercial Ship Builder, and Trader, Back-to-Africa Organizer

Paul Cuffee painting by Chester Harding
Source: Public Domain

1759: Born on the Quaker-owned Island of Cuttyhunk on January 17, Paul Cuffee (also spelled "Cuffe") was the seventh of ten children. Named "Paul Slocum" at birth, Paul's father was Kofi (Cuffee or Cuffe) Slocum, from the Ashanti Empire in West Africa[33]. He was first owned by Ebenezer Slocum of Dartmouth, MA, who, in 1742, sold him to John Slocum, also of Dartmouth. Three years later, John Slocum set Kofi free[34]. In

[33] https://www.blackpast.org/african-american-history/cuffe-paul-sr-1759-1817/

gratitude for his freedom, Kofi took the last name "Slocum". Paul's mother was Ruth Moses, an Aquinnah Wampanoag Indian[35].

1766: Kofi and Ruth bought 116 acres of land in Dartmouth, Massachusetts; this was highly unusual for a free Black man to do at the time.

1772: Kofi Slocum died in the spring of 1772; in his Last Will and Testament, he distributed his land holdings amongst his sons and referred to Paul and his siblings by the surname "Cuf" [36].

1776: While working on a whaling ship, the vessel was captured by the British. The crew, including Paul, was imprisoned for several months in New York. Upon his release he built his own ship and, avoiding the British blockades, plied a successful goods and services trade up and down the Eastern seaboard. Paul became an expert navigator and sea Captain.

1780: At the age of 21, Paul, his brother, and four freed Black men, alluding to taxation without representation, petitioned the courts to be accorded the same rights and privileges as other landholders who paid taxes[37]. In the petition, he referred to his brother and himself as Indian men. The House of

---

[34] https://paulcuffe.org/2020/05/12/the-remarkable-story-of-cuff-slocum/
[35] https://www.newenglandhistoricalsociety.com/paul-cuffe-back-africa-movement/
[36] https://paulcuffe.org/2020/05/12/the-remarkable-story-of-cuff-slocum/
[37] https://paulcuffe.org/biography/

Representatives denied the petition; however, the new State Constitution of Massachusetts added the Voting Reform Act which made property ownership a qualification to vote. In the meantime the brothers refused to pay their taxes and were incarcerated. Support from some influential people garnered their release and helped secure for them a reduction in their taxes.

1783: On February 25, Paul Cuffee married Alice Pequit, an Aquinnah Wampanoag Indian from a prominent family of Martha's Vineyard, and the widow of James Pequit[38]. In that same year, he and his brother-in-law, a Wampanoag Indian, launched a shipping business, which operated along the south coast of Massachusetts[39].

1787: Britain had established a settlement for freed Blacks desirous of returning to Africa; it was named "the Province of Freedom". The concept revolved around the idea of providing a place of opportunity for free blacks who wished to start a new life back in Africa. The designated colony was in Sierra Leone, and Freetown was the capital. This was expected to be a mecca for repatriated former slaves. Paul Cuffee believed the rights of Black people in America would not be realized and embraced this new plan[40].

---

[38] https://paulcuffe.org/biography/

[39] https://nha.org/research/nantucket-history/history-topics/who-was-paul-cuffe/

[40] https://www.newenglandhistoricalsociety.com/paul-cuffe-back-africa-movement/

1799: Cuffee acquired 140 acres of waterfront property in Westport, Massachusetts. At this point Paul Cuffee was the wealthiest African American and Native American in the United States. He also employed the most freed Blacks of any company in the U.S.

1807: The Trade Embargo Act was passed by Congress to restrict trade with Britain;

1812: Returning from Africa and Britain, unaware that the U.S. was at war with Great Britain, Cuffee's ships were seized for being in violation of the embargo. He went to the White House and met with President James Madison about the matter. It is said that Madison greeted Cuffee with affection; subsequently, his ships were returned to him. It is said Cuffee was the first person of color to enter the White House through the front door.

1811: Paul funded and opened the "Friendly Society of Sierra Leone". He led two expeditions crewed completely by Blacks to set up and open a trading culture in Sierra Leone. President Madison was also interested in the Back-to-Africa movement.

1815: Thirty-eight adults left America to settle in the new African colony. The cost was eight thousand dollars. Nevertheless, Paul Cuffee's vision of the Black man's return to Africa was not to be realized. The new immigrants were not met with open arms. The men were required to pledge allegiance to the British Crown and they refused. There was a fear of being drafted into military service. American Blacks, also, were against the idea.

1817: Three thousand attendees met at a Back-to Africa meeting of Bethel African Methodist Episcopal church under Richard Allen. The vote was a resounding "NO!" to the Back-to-Africa movement[41]. In a letter written by former friend and supporter James Forten, the collective answer to the Back-to-Africa movement declared, "The plan of colonizing is not asked for by us. We renounce and disclaim any connection with it." In another racially charged Back-to-Africa effort that year, Robert Finley, a White man, founded the well-funded American Colonization Society (ACS), which eclipsed Cuffee's efforts; the racist remarks coming from that organization eliminated any interest Cuffee may have had in joining forces with the ACS. That same year, in 1817, Paul Cuffee, in poor health from a difficult voyage in 1816, passed away at 69 years of age on September 7. He left an estate valued at twenty thousand dollars, worth approximately $419,000 in 2022[42]. His last words were "Let me pass quietly away".

[***NOTE:*** In the Twi language, which is spoken by the Ashanti people of Africa (modern-day Ghana), "Kofi" means "born on a Friday". Paul's father, Kofi, was 10 years old when he was stolen from his tribe in Western Africa. The Slocum family,

---

[41] https://www.newenglandhistoricalsociety.com/paul-cuffe-back-africa-movement/
[42] https://www.officialdata.org/us/inflation/1817?amount=20000

Quakers who owned Kofi, also owned Cuttyhunk Island, which was a part of the Elizabeth Island chain in Massachusetts. Paul's upbringing was in the Quaker tradition.

Kofi took the surname "Slocum" to honor the Quaker who owned him and subsequently freed him in 1745. At the time of his death, Kofi was already referring to his children's surname as "Cuf", a variation of his own name. Paul changed its spelling to "Cuffee".

The Library of Congress described the Back-to-Africa colonization movement as having roots in various plans first proposed in the 1700s:

"Some blacks supported emigration because they thought that black Americans would never receive justice in the United States. Others believed African-Americans should remain in the United States to fight against slavery and for full legal rights as American citizens. Some whites saw colonization as a way of ridding the nation of blacks, while others believed black Americans would be happier in Africa, where they could live free of racial discrimination. Still others believed black American colonists could play a central role in Christianizing and civilizing Africa"[43]. It was a contentious issue that, in the end, was not embraced by most freed Blacks of the day.]

---

[43] Library of Congress, The African American Mosaic: https://bit.ly/3A4HZqU

RICHARD ALLEN
[1760 – 1831]

Founder of the African Methodist Episcopal Church

Richard Allen
Source: Public Domain

1760: Allen was born into slavery in Philadelphia, Pennsylvania on February 14 to a wealthy Philadelphia merchant, Benjamin Chew[44]. He was referred to as "Negro Richard".

c. 1768: Along with his family, Allen was sold by his owner, Benjamin Chew, to a Delaware farmer, Stokeley Sturgis, and relocated to a Delaware farm.

[44] https://www.findagrave.com/memorial/23/richard-allen

1777: Allen became a Methodist after he was moved deeply by the words of a White traveling Methodist who preached against slavery. His owner was also converted and gave Allen the right to purchase his freedom; however, by this time, Sturgis had already sold Allen's mother and three of Allen's siblings.

1781: Allen began preaching as a circuit preacher in and around Delaware.

1783: He bought his freedom for $2,000 and adopted the surname "Allen". In 2022, the value of that sum would equal approximately $52,604[45].

1786: Allen attended St. George's Methodist Church and became an assistant minister, conducting services for Blacks. His praying was so powerful it influenced many other Blacks to attend the church. Though segregated seating was the norm in churches, that policy was not established in St. Georges until the late 1780s.

1787: St. Georges instituted segregated seating. At one service the Black parishioners sat in some new pews. During prayer they were told by a Trustee, "You must get up! You must not kneel here!"[46]. The Black congregants refused to relinquish their seats until the prayer was over then left the church *en masse*. This is

[45] https://www.officialdata.org/us/inflation/1783?amount=2000
[46] https://christianhistoryinstitute.org/magazine/article/you-must-not-kneel-here

thought to be the first demonstration against discrimination by Blacks in America.

1787: Richard Allen, Absalom Jones and several others formed the Free African Society (FAS) in Philadelphia. As a religious non-denominational mutual-aid organization, for the most part, it provided help to other Blacks[47].

1793: Yellow Fever struck. Blacks were called to aid Whites during the epidemic. Many Blacks were nurses who provided aid, knowing Whites were using them in order to save their own lives. That year, a White publisher in Philadelphia, Richard Carey, published a pamphlet accusing Blacks of profiteering off the epidemic and plundering the households of Whites while pretending to help them. Richard Allen and Benjamin Rush wrote and published "*A Narrative of the Proceedings of Black People*" in an attempt to refute Carey's lies.

1794: Allen and other Black Methodists established the Bethel Church in an old Blacksmith's shop. According to biography.com,

> Bethel Church became known as "Mother Bethel" because it eventually birthed the African Methodist Episcopal Church. Helped by his second wife Sarah, Allen also helped to hide escaped enslaved people, as the

---

[47] https://www.biography.com/religious-figure/richard-allen

basement of the Bethel Church was a stop on the Underground Railroad. (para. 7)

1799: Allen became the first ordained Black minister in the Methodist Episcopal Church.

1816: After years of opposition by the White Methodists, Allen sued for the right of AME Church to exist as an institution independent of the (White) Methodist Church, and to keep its property. He won both cases[48].

Several Black Methodist Churches that had been opened by that time came together and formed their own hierarchy independent of the original (White) Methodist Conference. Allen was ordained Bishop and was thus the first Black Bishop in America.

1830: The National Negro Convention Movement, an open forum for abolitionists, activists, and Black leaders, was formed.

1831: On March 26, Richard Allen died at his home on Spruce Street in Philadelphia, PA; he was interred beneath Bethel Church in Philadelphia[49].

---

[48] https://www.ame-church.com/our-church/our-history/
[49] https://www.findagrave.com/memorial/23/richard-allen

JAMES DERHAM
[1762 – 1802?]

First Black Physician Allowed to Practice without a Medical Degree

James Derham.
Source: Public Domain

1762: Derham was born, enslaved, in Philadelphia.

1762-1776: Derham was taught to read and write and received instructions in Christianity. He had several owners, three of whom were Physicians. In this medical environment, he not only became literate, but he also showed an affinity for the practice of medicine. In addition to English, he also became fluent in French, spoke Spanish adequately, and learned the basics of Pharmacy and caring for patients under Dr. John Kearsley, Jr., the first physician to own him.

1776: After the death of Kearsley, Derham was sold to Dr. George West[50] who furthered his instructions in medicine. Dr. West was Surgeon to the Sixth British Regiment. During the Revolutionary War, Derham performed many menial tasks related to the practice of medicine but continued to learn and gain knowledge in the profession.

1783: After the Revolutionary War, Derham was sold to Dr. Robert Dove and moved to New Orleans[51]. Dove allowed Derham to practice on patients, regardless of color. This was the first known instance of a Black American administering to non-Blacks. Dr. Dove's esteem and admiration for Derham grew and, after three years, Dove consented to grant Derham his freedom.

1783: Dove freed Derham under favorable terms and, under Dove's patronage, Derham developed his own practice, focusing on the throat. He was so successful that Dr. Benjamin Rush, the preeminent physician of the time, offered to help him set up in Philadelphia. Derham declined and remained in Louisiana.

1789: Derham helped save many lives during the Yellow Fever epidemic and was said to have saved more lives than any other physician in colonial Philadelphia.

---

[50] https://www.journals.uchicago.edu/doi/pdf/10.2307/3035633
[51] https://www.ncbi.nlm.nih.gov/pmc/articles/PMC2621656/pdf/jnma00852-0052.pdf

1801: Due to newly established regulations, he was restricted in the practice of medicine as he did not have a formal medical degree; nevertheless, he continued to practice medicine[52].

1802: James Derham disappeared under mysterious circumstances, and his whereabouts have never been ascertained.

[52] https://bit.ly/3uG5LqG

DENMARK VESEY
[1767–1822]

Self-educated, Insurrectionist

Denmark Vesey Monument - Hampton Park - Charleston SC

c. 1767: The exact date and place of Denmark Vesey's birth cannot be stated with certainty[53]; however, reports are that he was born around 1767, possibly on the island of St. Thomas, Danish West Indies[54].

1781: Denmark was sold to Joseph Vesey, a Bermuda slaver captain and was given Vesey's surname.

---

[53] https://www.nps.gov/people/denmark-vesey.htm
[54] https://www.britannica.com/biography/Denmark-Vesey

1783: Vesey and his owner settled in Charleston, South Carolina (SC).

1799-1800: By now a self-educated man, in 1800 Vesey won a lottery in the sum of $1,500 in an East Bay Street lottery and bought his freedom for $600[55]; subsequently, he became a successful carpenter. By this time, Vesey knew about the slave revolts in Haiti, which had occurred in the 1790s, and began to read anti-slavery literature. He began envisioning a slave revolt to free enslaved Blacks in America.

1815: Fearful of Haitian inspired revolts, Whites began interrupting church services of Black worshippers, accusing them of collecting monies to purchase the freedom of slaves. They even sought to erect buildings over a cemetery for Black people.

1817: Several thousand Black worshippers left White churches and established an African Methodist Episcopal (AME) church.

1818: Whites interrupted a church service, arresting 140 parishioners. Denmark Vesey had become a leader and strong voice in the church and was tiring of the unequal treatment of enslaved and free Blacks. Vesey's thoughts turned to rebellion and he planned on leading a slave rebellion in the United States; however, the plot was exposed.

---

[55] https://bit.ly/3CXEum3

1822: For his efforts to ignite a rebellion, Vesey died by hanging in Charleston, South Carolina[56].

[***NOTE:*** Inspired by the success of the Haitian revolt of 1791, Vesey hatched a plan to attack arsenals, seize weapons, kill the slaveholders, and capture the city of Charleston[57]. The date of the planned slave rebellion was June 16, 1822. George Wilson, an AME member who identified more with his masters, revealed the plot. Vesey and others were arrested.

In a retrospective look at the event, the Yorkville Enquirer, Yorkville, SC, reported on July 25, 1922 that Vesey and 34 others were executed[58]; and "43 others transported"[59].Vesey was hanged for the planned uprising, which was estimated to involve 9,000 slaves and 2 years preparation. Between June and August of 1822, 131 people were charged as conspirators, 67 of them were incarcerated, and 35 or more were hanged. George Wilson gained his freedom as a result of his betrayal of the planned uprising. He went insane and eventually committed suicide.]

---

[56] http://crdl.usg.edu/people/v/vesey_denmark_ca_1767_1822/?Welcome

[57] https://www.britannica.com/biography/Denmark-Vesey

[58] https://bit.ly/3CXEum3

[59] Presumably "transported" meant transportation to one of the plantations in the Caribbean, which were reputed to a virtual death sentence as conditions there were harsher and far crueler than in the U.S.A.

JARENA LEE
[1783 –1849]

Preacher, Missionary

Jarena Lee
Source: Public Domain

1783: Jarena Lee was born free to free Black parents at Cape May, New Jersey, on February 11[60].

1790: From the age of seven, she worked as an in-residence domestic servant to the Sharp family. In her teens, she relocated to Philadelphia doing housework. This move separated her from her family.

---

[60] https://bit.ly/3Eb5aRu

1803: Lee was a deeply spiritual woman, having wrestled with sin and forgiveness almost to the point of her own self-destruction; however, she came to peace when she became a Christian. Feeling a deep need for God and a deep sense of her sinfulness, Jarena began attending an Episcopal church after leaving a previous Church feeling spiritually bereft. However, she found herself totally disconnected from the Episcopalians, as they were segregated and aloof.

1807: Lee joined Bethel AME[61] and was baptized. She requested and was denied the right to preach by Bishop Allen[62]. At the time, Protestant churches followed a "let your women keep silent in the churches" theology. Her response to this initial denial reminded church leaders that men preach because Jesus died and was the Savior of all: "Is He not a whole Savior, instead of a half-one?"[63] she asked.

Bishop Richard Allen changed his position and granted her license to preach; thus, Lee was the first woman preacher in the AME Church.

1832: She became a traveling missionary preaching all over the Eastern United States and Canada[64]. She evangelized people of all colors, living on handouts for transportation and places to sleep for she was not given a salary.

---

[61] African Methodist Episcopalian Church
[62] https://www.pbs.org/wgbh/aia/part3/3h1638.html
[63] https://www.nyhistory.org/
[64] https://librarycompany.org/women/portraits_religion/lee.htm

1836: Lee published an autobiographical account of her religious and missionary work.

1839: She became an abolitionist and was active in the American Antislavery Society.

1849: An updated version of Lee's 1836 autobiography "The Life and Religious Experience of Jarena Lee" was published.

c. 1850: The exact date of her death remains in question; however, her burial site is reputed to be at the Pisgah AME Church in Lawnside, NJ.

THOMAS L. JENNINGS [1791-1856]

Inventor, Tailor, Abolitionist; First African American to be Awarded a US Patent

Thomas Jennings.
Source: Public Domain

1791: Born free in New York, NY, Jennings became a successful tailor, and began working on a cleaning product to add to the services he provided.

1821: Jennings was the first Black person to receive a patent, which was for a process he called "dry scouring" using chemicals and very little water to remove dirt and grime from clothing[65]; this process was a precursor to modern dry cleaning. He was 29 years old at the time and his success enabled him to purchase his family's freedom. By law, slaves could not get a patent as they, and the fruits of their labor, were considered the property of their owners.

1831: An abolitionist who was active in civil rights for Blacks, Jennings was appointed as assistant secretary to the First Annual National Negro Convention, which was held in Philadelphia, PA.

1854: Jennings sued the Third Avenue Rail Road Company of New York for evicting his daughter, Elizabeth Jennings, from a streetcar roughly, causing her bodily injury[66]. He hired an all-white firm, *Culver, Parker, and Arthur*, also of New York, to represent his daughter in court. Chester A. Arthur, the junior partner in the law firm and 24 years old at the time, represented Elizabeth Jennings.

1855: Elizabeth Jennings won the case and was awarded a total of $247.50 in damages; additionally, the Third Avenue Rail Road Company decided to desegregate their streetcars. Together with James McCune Smith and Rev. James W.C. Pennington, Thomas Jennings founded the Legal Rights Association that year[67].

---

[65] https://www.smithsonianmag.com/innovation/first-african-american-hold-patent-invented-dry-scouring-180971394/
[66] https://history.nycourts.gov/case/jennings-third-ave/

1859: Thomas Jennings died on February 12 in Manhattan, New York County, and was buried in the Cypress Hills Cemetery, Kings County, Brooklyn, New York.

[***NOTE:*** Chester A. Arthur eventually went on to become the 21st President of America (1881-1885)].

[67] https://aaregistry.org/story/thomas-jennings-born/

ALEXANDER L. TWILIGHT [1795 –1857]

State Legislator, Educator, Clergyman

Alexander Twilight.
Source: Public Domain

1795: On September 23, Alexander Lucius Twilight was born of mixed parentage in either Bradford or Corinth, Vermont (VT). His mother, Mary Twilight, was either White, or very fair-skinned, while his father was of mixed race[68]. In fact, for most of his life, Twilight was recorded as being "White" on US Census records[69].

[68] https://www.middlebury.edu/office/twilight-project/bio
[69] https://www.usatoday.com/in-depth/news/2021/02/08/complex-history-alexander-twilight-middleburys-first-black-graduate/4094045001/

1803: From the age of eight, Twilight farmed for a neighbor to earn money for grammar school; he was an indentured servant until 1816.

1816: He obtained his freedom at age 21.

1821 - 23: He graduated from Middlebury College and, of the 28 men to receive the BA degree. He was the first Black person to graduate from a college. He became a schoolteacher in Peru, NY.

1826: Twilight married Mercy Ladd Merrill of Unity, New Hampshire. He became a clergyman, ordained in the Congregational Ministries.

1836: He was the first Black American elected to a state legislature. Twilight was a member of the General Assembly of the State of Vermont. He opened *Athenian hall*, a boarding school with 14 dorm rooms, at Brownington Center Road at Derby Line, Brownington Center, Orleans County, VT; today, it is The Old Stone House Museum, VT[70,71].

1847: Unknown conflicts led to Twilight's leaving both teaching and preaching for a while. He lived in Canada for 5 years.

1852: He returned to Brownington, VT, where he taught until 1855.

---

[70] https://www.loc.gov/item/vt0048/

[71] https://www.oldstonehousemuseum.org/twilight-tidbit-one/

1855: Twilight suffered a stroke, which partially paralyzed him; consequently, he quit teaching for good.

1857: Alexander L. Twilight died in Brownington, VT and was buried in the Brownington Village Cemetery (Congregational) in Brownington Village, Orleans County, VT.

[***NOTE:*** The reader is encouraged to peruse the website of the Old Stonehouse Museum[72] for a more in-depth look at the life of this remarkable African American.]

[72] https://www.oldstonehousemuseum.org/twilight-tidbit-one

SOJOURNER TRUTH
[1797–1883]

Abolitionist, Freedom Fighter, Minister, Women's Rights Activist, Author

Sojourner Truth
Source: Public Domain

c. 1797: Named "Isabella Baumfree" at birth, Sojourner Truth was born on Colonel Johannes Hardenbergh's estate, to James and Elizabeth Baumfree who were enslaved to Hardenbergh, a Dutch settler in Swartekill[73], Ulster County, New York (NY). She was one of 10 or 12 children[74], and grew up speaking Dutch.

[73] Swartekill was renamed "Rifton Glen" by Jeremiah W. Dimick in 1861.
[74] According to the Encyclopedia Britannica, Sojourner Truth's legal name was Isabella Van Wagener. Most likely, she took the Van Wagener name after they

Her enslaved father was captured in Ghana, which was named the "Gold Coast" at the time of his captivity. Her mother was a descendant of enslaved people from Guinea.

1799: New York gradually abolished slavery for future generations of slaves born after 1799, but left intact the enslavement of all those born before 1799[75]; Isabella was born two years earlier, in 1797.

1806: Isabella was nine years old when Colonel Hardenbergh died. Hardenbergh's son auctioned her off to John Neely of Kingston, NY, for $100 and a flock of sheep[76]. Neely was very abusive to her.

1808: She was sold for $105 to a tavern owner, Martinus Schryver, also of Kingston, NY. Mrs. Schryver continued the abuse.

1810: At age 13, she was sold to John Dumont, and labored for him for 17 years[77]. She was badly treated by his wife.

1815: Baumfree fell in love with an enslaved man, Robert, from another farm. Robert was beaten to death by his owner when he disobeyed his owner's orders not to meet with Isabella;

---

bought her from the last of her enslavers and set her free. Still later, she changed her name to the appellation by which she is known today.

[75] https://history.nycourts.gov/when-did-slavery-end-in-new-york/

[76] https://www.nps.gov/people/sojourner-truth.htm

[77] https://www.notablebiographies.com/St-Tr/Truth-Sojourner.html

subsequently, she was forced to marry an older slave named Thomas, with whom she had three children[78].

Altogether, Baumfree gave birth to five children: her firstborn, James, died in childbirth; a daughter, Diana (born in 1815), resulted from rape by Dumont. Peter (born in 1821), Elizabeth (born in 1825), and Sophia (born in 1826) were the children of Thomas.

1817: A law was passed in NY that granted freedom to all slaves born before July 4, 1799; however, they were to be freed by 1827. Children would be indentured servants until age 21; Baumfree fell into this group. This law made NY the first state to abolish slavery fully.

1826: Dumont had promised Isabella that he would free her one year before the NY emancipation date of 1827; however, he reneged on his promise to her. Learning that he planned to sell her, she escaped taking her youngest daughter, Sophia, with her. She went to the home of two Quakers, Isaac and Maria Van Wagenen, who, after compensating Dumont $20 for Isabella's services, promptly set her free. Isabella's emancipation would have been eight months later. Dumont sold her young son, illegally, to a plantation owner in Alabama. Baumfree sued Dumont in court and won; her son was returned to her in 1828[79].

---

[78] https://www.nps.gov/people/sojourner-truth.htm
[79] https://www.britannica.com/biography/Sojourner-Truth

This was the first case of a Black woman suing a White man and winning.

1828: She moved to New York City and was baptized into Christianity during the Second Great Awakening; she also became a successful and sought after speaker.

1835: Baumfree worked for two of the leaders in a cult-like spiritual organization called *The Kingdom*. Rivalry between the two leaders ended in murder when one of them, Matthias, killed the other, Elijah Pierson. Baumfree was named as an accomplice, but was found innocent. After that, she worked as a house-servant in New York City for the next eight years. When a White couple accused her of theft and trying to poison them, she sued them for slander and won the case. She was the first Black person to win such a case against a White person[80].

1843: Baumfree became a Methodist. In June, answering what she felt was a call to preach and to fight against slavery, which was still in effect in the Southern states, Baumfree changed her name to Sojourner Truth; her name change reflected her new mission in life. She traveled throughout New England preaching and holding prayer sessions in churches and camp meetings at which she drew large crowds.

1844: Sojourner moved to Northampton, Massachusetts, and joined the Northampton Association of Education and Industry, a

---

[80] https://www.notablebiographies.com/St-Tr/Truth-Sojourner.html

new program started by abolitionists in Massachusetts. Through the program she met other abolitionists and activists such as Frederick Douglass and William Lloyd Garrison. The Association disbanded in 1846.

1850: She dictated her memoirs to Oliver Gilbert who published her autobiography "The Narrative of Sojourner Truth: a Northern Slave". With proceeds from the sale of the book, she bought a house in Northampton, MA, and paid it off in three years by selling photographs of herself with the caption "I sell the shadow to support the substance." [81]

1851: At the first National Women's Rights Convention in Ohio, Sojourner was the main speaker. It was here she gave her now famous speech, "*Ain't I a Woman?*" Slavery had so degraded the position of Black women they were thought of as having practically no value. In her speech, she stated, "Among Blacks are women, among the women there Are Blacks".

1857: Truth moved to Harmonia, Michigan (MI), closer to her daughter; later she moved to Battle Creek, MI.

1864: During the Civil War, she helped recruit Black men to join the Union army. She worked for the National Freedmen's Association in Washington DC, which provided food, clothes and whatever they could to the displaced Blacks. While at the Association, Truth met With President Lincoln. She

[81] https://www.nps.gov/people/sojourner-truth.htm

advocated for the desegregation of streetcars, while using them in all her travels around town.

1870: Truth met with President Grant and advocated for land for freed Black Americans; she continued this effort for years but Congress never acted on it. Once active in women's suffrage, Sojourner withdrew her support when Susan B. Anthony would not support a Black man's right to vote if women didn't have the right to vote.

1883: Sojourner Truth died at 86 years of age on November 26, at Battle Creek, Calhoun County, Michigan (MI). She is buried at Oak Hill Cemetery in Battle Creek, MI.

[***NOTE:*** In 1997 NASA chose the name "Sojourner" for the first robot that would explore Mars[82]. The asteroid 249521 was named "Truth".

2009: Sojourner Truth was the first Black woman to be honored with a self-portrait bust in the US Capitol building.]

---

[82] https://mars.nasa.gov/MPF/rover/name.html

JEREMIAH G. "JERRY" HAMILTON [1806–1875]

Wall Street Broker, First Black Wall Street Millionaire a.k.a. the Prince of Darkness

Jeremiah Jerry Hamilton
Source: Public Domain

c. 1806-1807: Hamilton's parents were born in Haiti; however, the place of his birth is not known for certain, and reports are that he may have been born in Haiti or Richmond, Virginia, on August 21[83]. Nothing is known of him until 1828.

[83] https://aaregistry.org/story/jeremiah-hamilton-financier-born/

1828: After participating in a failed counterfeit coinage scam, Hamilton fled Haiti and headed for America with his White cohorts.

1833: He assumed a new identity, "Jerry Hamilton", and embarked on a very successful trading career as a Wall Street broker.

1835: The Great Fire of New York destroyed New York City's financial district[84]. Hamilton seized on the opportunity to amass a great fortune by swindling several of its victims.

1843: The NY District Attorney (NYDA) charged Hamilton with conspiring to defraud the Atlantic Insurance Company (AIC) of $50,000. Hamilton was accused of over-insuring shipping vessels, and then destroying them deliberately[85]. The NYDA dropped the case after Hamilton charged the AIC with hiring goons to lure him to the North River to drown him.

1845: By this time, all of the marine insurance companies in NY had organized and agreed collectively never to insure any vessel that involved Hamilton. The New York Stock Exchange (NYSE) unsuccessfully threatened its members with expulsion if they did not stop doing business with Hamilton. At the same time, Hamilton developed a new system in which investors pooled their monies; he served as their agent to borrow more money in

---

[84] https://www.history.com/news/great-fire-new-york-1835

[85] https://www.theatlantic.com/business/archive/2015/10/wall-street-first-black-millionaire/411622/

order to invest in stocks of his choosing. The risky plan gave him great financial power and resembled what is known today as a *Hedge Fund.* Hamilton was famous for filing claims against businesses where he had purchased shares, forcing them to dissolve and redistribute assets to their shareholders.

1850s: Hamilton fought one of the most ruthless and successful businessmen, Cornelius Vanderbilt, for control of the Accessory Transit Company. The victory went to Vanderbilt, who acknowledged Hamilton's skills with respect.

Jerry Hamilton managed over 12 million dollars in business interests and only did business with Whites.

1863: During the Draft Riots[86], an Irish mob overran his NY residence on East 29th Street intending to hang him; he escaped through a window.

1875: Jerry Hamilton died of pneumonia at age 68 or 69 on May 19 in New York, NY[87] , and was buried in the Green-Wood Cemetery in Kings County, Brooklyn, NY[88]. At the time of his death, he had amassed a fortune of over two million dollars[89].

[***NOTE:*** According to the New York Times (2013), the historical archives contain copious news reports about Hamilton; the

---

86 https://www.history.com/topics/american-civil-war/draft-riots
87 https://www.wikitree.com/wiki/Hamilton-13232
88 https://www.findagrave.com/memorial/114409167/jeremiah-g.-hamilton
89 In 2022, two million dollars was worth over $50.5 million dollars (https://www.officialdata.org/us/inflation/1875?amount=2000000)

publication listed over 50 court cases in which he was involved. Yet, although Hamilton was a very prominent figure in the financial world of the 1800s, he has been largely ignored by modern American historians; in fact, although many images of the wealthy financier must have existed, the image shown in this article may not be that of Hamilton as few, if any, seems to have survived.

Hamilton was such a brilliant, notorious, and ruthless con artist and schemer that he came to be known as the *Prince of Darkness*. He lived a double life as a wealthy, successful Wall Street broker married to a White woman, and that of a second-class person of color. White racists hated him because of his success and his White spouse.

At one point, Hamilton suggested, brazenly, that quality champagne and good cigars were the ways satisfied clients should show him their appreciation. Nevertheless, he was admired for his financial shrewdness, judgment, and business skills and, although he battled Cornelius Vanderbilt in court and lost, Vanderbilt privately praised Hamilton's business expertise.]

GEORGE T. DOWNING
[1819 –1905]

Abolitionist, Activist, Entrepreneur, Restaurateur

George T. Downing
Source: Public Domain

1819: George Thomas Downing was born to Thomas Downing and Rebecca Downing (formerly "West") in New York County (Manhattan), NY, on December 30. As his father was a successful restaurateur, Downing, the first-born of five children, was born into wealth.

1830s: During his teenage years and throughout his adulthood up to the Civil War, Downing became active in the Underground Railroad (UR) helping to free fugitive Blacks from their enslavement in the slave-holding states. His father's restaurants were stops along the UR.

1833: At the young age of 14, Downing and a few of his friends established a literary society that focused on discussions about the conditions of Blacks. They took a moral stance against celebrating the fourth of July, asserting it was a mockery to the Black race[90].

1841: Downing was a delegate to the first convention of the American Reform Board of Disenfranchised Commissioners NY Legislature. He lobbied for equal rights.

1842: He built a successful catering business in NY.

1846: Downing opened a branch of his father's Oyster House in Newport, Rhode Island (RI).

1847: He became a member of the first Board of Trustees in the New York Society for the Protection of Colored Children.

1850: Downing expanded his catering and restaurant business to Mathewson Street, Providence, RI.

1854: He built the Girt Hotel, a luxury hotel in Newport catering to Whites only, which an arsonist destroyed.

---

[90]https://www.encyclopedia.com/african-american-focus/news-wires-white-papers-and-books/downing-george-t

1857: He began a nine-year campaign in Rhode Island to end segregation in Bristol, Newport, and Providence[91].

1860: He built the Downing Block; in 1865 the location became a naval hospital.

1865: For 12 years Downing headed the Refectory for the House of Representatives.

1866: Downing's efforts to end segregation were successful and the General Assembly voted to end segregation in public schools by an overwhelming margin.

1869: He helped organize the Colored National Labor Union.

1873: He helped gain passage of the Public Accommodations Law in Washington, DC.

1880s: He became disillusioned with the Republicans. He was also upset that his people would, without question, support one party. Downing eventually returned to RI, continuing his activist efforts. His restaurant had been a station in the Underground Railroad system.

1889: He helped to organize the Colored National Labor Union.

1903: George T. Downing died and is buried at Island Cemetery, Newport, Newport County, Rhode Island[92]. He spent his life

---

[91]http://www.riheritagehalloffame.org/inductees_detail.cfm?iid=471
[92] https://www.findagrave.com/memorial/119861600/george-thomas-downing

successfully, in some instances, bettering the lives of Black Americans. He was considered a man of grit and high moral standards.

JOSHUA MCCARTER SIMPSON [1820? –1876]

Abolitionist, Poet/Singer, Herbal Doctor, Underground Railroad Director

Joshua M. Simpson.
Source: Public Domain

c.1820: Simpson was born in indentured servitude in McConnelsville, Morgan County, Ohio (OH), became free at 21 years of age, and was self-taught and literate; from a young age, he harbored deep feelings about the condition of Black people.

1844-1848: Simpson attended—and graduated from—Oberlin Collegiate Institute, becoming an herbal doctor and a grocer. He began writing poetry, setting his poems to the meter of popular songs, and singing the verses of his poems to those melodies. He realized he could sing aloud what he could not speak aloud.

1842: He was the first composer of overtly anti-slavery songs and published books of anti-slavery poem-songs. He sang with clarity, insight, courage, and fearlessness. He sang one of his poems, *To The White People Of America*, to the tune of *Massas in the Cold, Cold Grave.*

1874: Simpson put together two decades of work comprised of 53 songs and published it. He chose popular tunes and hymns to use in singing the words. Fugitive slaves sang many of his songs on the Underground Railroad. One of his songs, *Away to Canada*, was a popular abolitionist song. His collection of poem-songs, titled *The Emancipation Car*, was penned specifically for the Underground Railroad.

1876: Joshua McCarter Simpson died at age 55 or 56 in Zanesville, Muskingum County, OH. His burial site is at the Greenwood Cemetery, Muskingum, OH. The extent of his works was unknown until recently.

ALEXANDER T. AUGUSTA [1825 – 1890]

Physician – War Veteran

Alexander T. Augusta
Source: Public Domain

1825: Alexander T. Augusta was born free to free Black parents. One of the gifts of freedom was access to literacy. Augusta pursued higher education seeking to become a physician, while earning his living as a barber. He applied to the University of Pennsylvania and was denied admission because he was not White; however, a member of the faculty at Pennsylvania tutored him privately.

1856: He graduated with an MB University of Toronto, Canada.

1856: He was the first Black chief administrator of Toronto City Hospital.

1862: In the US, Augusta requested to serve Black troops fighting in the Union Army

1862: He received a presidential commission from President Lincoln.

1863: He entered service as a Major and the first Black doctor. Augusta had the highest military rank given an African American to date. He was not accepted as a leader among White doctors and their resistance caused Augusta to be reassigned. He went to the Freedman's Hospital where he rose to Chief of Staff.

1864: Whites viciously forced him off the Capital streetcar. Senator Charles Sumner heard about the incident and brought it before Congress. The Congress decreed all Capital streetcars to be non-segregated.

1865: Augusta's military service ended. He left the Union Army a Lt. Colonel.

1868: He returned to Howard University and was the first African American on staff as a member of the medical faculty at a University in the US.

1869-71: Augusta was the first Black awarded two honorary degrees.

1884: He founded the first Black medical association: the Medico-Chirurgical Society.

1890: Dr. Alexander T. Augusta died; a monument was erected for him at Arlington National Cemetery—the very first for a Black man[93].

[***NOTE:*** During the Civil War, Dr. Augusta fought for pay equity for Black soldiers. According to the National Park Services site, "During this time, all enlisted men of color were paid $7 a month, the standard wage for a Black private. White privates received $13 a month. As a commissioned officer, Augusta was initially salaried at $169 per month, the compensation of an army surgeon holding the rank of major. But this changed in early 1864 when the Army paymaster refused to pay him more than $7 per month. Augusta rejected this indignation."

Dr. Augusta was one of the medical personnel present at President Abraham Lincoln's side as the President was dying from a gunshot wound to the head.]

---

[93]The National Park Services: https://www.nps.gov/foth/learn/historyculture/alexander-augusta.htm

Dr. REBECCA L. DAVIS CRUMPLER [1831–1895]

Physician, Nurse, Author

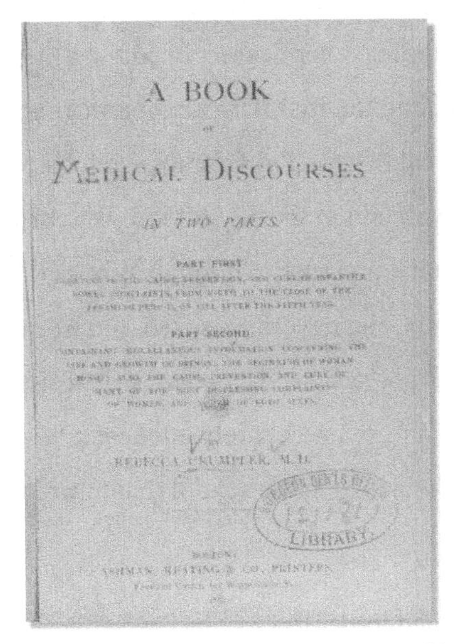
A BOOK

MEDICAL DISCOURSES

IN TWO PARTS

PART FIRST

PART SECOND

BY

REBECCA CRUMPLER, M.D.

LIBRARY

No known image of Dr. Crumpler exists. This is a cover image of the first medical book known to be published by a Black doctor in the U.S.A

1831: Rebecca Davis was born free in Delaware to Absolum and Matilda (Webber) Davis[94]. She lived with her aunt in Pennsylvania who spent time caring for sick neighbors[95].

[94] https://www.blackpast.org/african-american-history/crumpler-rebecca-davis-lee-1831-1895/
[95] https://cfmedicine.nlm.nih.gov/physicians/biography_73.html

1852: Davis was living and working as a nurse in Massachusetts (MA).

1860: She entered New England Female Medical College on scholarship.

1863: Her Scholarship was revoked; however, she won tuition from Wade Scholarship Fund.

1864: Davis completed her degree, becoming the only Black female to do so, and the first African American female to be awarded a medical degree. Dr. Crumpler relocated to Richmond VA to help provide aid to the 30,000 free Blacks who were under serious racial pressure. Although Whites disregarded her and her profession, she nevertheless worked in various venues with other Black physicians. The board was resistant to awarding her degree claiming she was barely adequate; however, she excelled in mathematics in the school that awarded her a scholarship.

1869: She returned to Boston.

1883: Crumpler published the *Book of Medical Discourses*, which proffered advice for women and children. It was the first medical book published by a Black female doctor.

1895: On March 9, Rebecca Crumpler died in the Hyde Park section of Boston; she was buried in nearby Fairview Cemetery. There are no known pictures of her.

[***NOTE:*** Before working as a nurse in MA (1851), Rebecca attended the West Newton English and Classical Private School and was enrolled as a “special student”. She was the first African American female doctor in the U.S. and authored the first medical book by an African American.]

JOSEPH HAYNE RAINEY [1832 – 1887]

U.S. Member House of Representatives, Republican

Joseph Hayne Rainey
Source: Public Domain

1832: Joseph H. Rainey was born to enslaved parents in Georgetown, South Carolina (SC). His father, a barber, bought the family's freedom after saving the money he was allowed to retain. Rainey also became a barber.

1861: At the start of the Civil War, Rainey was drafted into the Confederate Army as a manual laborer.

1862: Rather than help the cause of the Confederate states, he and his wife fled to Bermuda.

1866: At the end of the Civil War, Rainey returned to SC, moving a year later to Georgetown, where he helped form the Republican Party.

1870: Rainey was sworn in as the first Black American to serve as a U.S. Representative in Congress[96], filling a vacancy left by B. Franklin Whittemore[97]. He backed passage of an amnesty bill for former Confederates and the Civil Rights Act of 1875[98]and was re-elected to four more terms in the newly formed Republican Party. Among his African American contemporaries, Rainey's was the longest tenure in the House of Representatives during Reconstruction.

1876: Democrats took control of the House of Representatives, but Rainey won in a contested election.

1878: Rainey lost his bid for re-election to the House of Representatives to a Democrat, which ended his political aspirations.

1879: President Rutherford B. Hayes appointed Rainey a United States Internal Revenue Agent in South Carolina.

---

[96] https://history.house.gov/People/Listing/R/RAINEY,-Joseph-Hayne-(R000016)/

[97] https://www.hmdb.org/m.asp?m=102552

[98] https://www.southcarolinapublicradio.org/show/south-carolina-from-a-to-z/2021-01-18/r-is-for-rainey-joseph-hayne-1832-1887

1887: On August 1, Joseph Rainey died of congestive fever at the age of 54 in Georgetown, SC. His burial site is in Baptist Cemetery, Georgetown County, SC[99].

[***NOTE***: In his position on the U.S. House Committee of Freedmen's Affairs of 1865, Rainey fought for protection for Black Americans—especially from the Klu Klux Klan. Then President Grant passed the Klu Klux Klan Act supposedly to address their burning and lynching of Blacks on a whim. The passage of the Act made no difference in the Klan's behavior. Rainey also fought for the interests of other minorities such as Native American Indians and Chinese immigrants.]

[99] https://politicalgraveyard.com/geo/SC/GO-buried.html

BASS REEVES
[1838 –1910]

Federal Deputy, U.S. Marshall

Bass Reeves
Source: Public Domain

1838: Born enslaved to William S. Reeves in Crawford County, Arkansas (AR), in July 1838[100], details about Bass Reeves's early life are vague.

1846: William Reeves moved his family and slaves to Grayson County, Texas (TX).

[100] https://encyclopediaofarkansas.net/entries/bass-reeves-1747/

1861 -186 5: Reeves claimed to have fought under his owner's son during the Civil War, on the side of the Confederacy, until 1863. However, his family members maintained that, after a fight with his owner in 1861 or 1862, Bass fled and hid among the Creek and Seminole Indians in Indian Territory, modern day Kansas (KS) and Oklahoma (OK)[101]. The Indian Territory was a haven for criminals.

1875: Reeves, one of the first of 200 lawmen hired by Judge Isaac C. Parker as commissioned Deputy U.S. Marshals covering Western Arkansas and the Indian Territory[102], became the first Black federal lawman west of the Mississippi River[103]. As a U.S. Marshal in Indian Territory, he had the power to arrest Whites, which, for a Black man, was highly unusual. In addition to his duties as a commissioned Deputy Marshal, he sometimes worked as a posse man with more seasoned federal officers. He was tall and able-bodied; a capable rider in the posse and an expert marksman with a preference for his Winchester rifle. He was known to wear disguises and engage in subterfuge. According to reports, to capture four criminals who were hiding in a cabin, Reeves got a hay wagon and dressed as a farmer. He pretended his wagon was stuck. When the men came out to help he arrested them.

---

[101] https://www.britannica.com/biography/Bass-Reeves
[102] The Indian Territory was comprised of the Cherokee, Chocktaw, Chickasaw, Creek, and Seminole nations (https://www.nps.gov/fosm/learn/historyculture/bass_reeves.htm)
[103] https://www.history.com/news/bass-reeves-real-lone-ranger-a-black-man

1886: Reeves was indicted for murdering his cook in 1885. Good lawyers and murky witnesses resulted in his acquittal.

1907: Reeves was removed from federal service when Oklahoma became a state; subsequently, he was hired by the Muskogee Police Department, where he worked for two years before retiring. It was rumored there was no criminal activity on his beat.

1910: On 12 January Bass Reeves died of Bright's disease, aged 71, in Muscogee, Oklahoma. He is buried in Agency Cemetery, OK.

[***NOTE***: Reeves was reputed to be a man of very high morals and arrested his own son for murdering his wife; his son spent several years in prison.]

BLANCHE KELSO BRUCE [1841–1898]

Reconstruction Era United States Senator (R), Mississippi

Portrait of Sen. Blanche Kelso Bruce by Simmie Knox[104]

1841: On March 1, in Prince Edward County, West Virginia (WV), Blanche Kelso Bruce was born of an enslaved mother, Polly Bruce, and a White planter father, Pettus Perkinson[105], son-in-law to the deceased Lemuel Bruce, a slave-owning planter who owned Bruce's mother. While there are reports that Bruce was treated very kindly by Perkinson, there are other reports that he was made to pick cotton at eight years old, and endured many

[104]Portrait commissioned by the U.S. Senate. U.S. Senate Collection (cat.no. 32.00039.000

[105]https://history.house.gov/People/Detail/10029

whippings[106]. He was a servant to his half brother, William Perkinson. William may have taught him to read and write, or he may have benefitted from William's tutors[107, 108].

1849: Perkinson moved the plantation operation to Mississippi.

1861: During the U.S. Civil War, Bruce ran away to Kansas (KS) where he attempted to join the Union Army, but was denied admittance. He settled in Lawrence, KS, where he taught school[109].

1864: He opened the first school for Black children in Hannibal, Missouri (MO), eventually moving to Mississippi and there began his political career.

1869: He was appointed a supervisor of elections in Mississippi.

1870 - 1874: With support from White Republicans, in 1870, he was made Registrar of Voters in Jackson, MS, Tallahatchie county. This was the beginning of his history-making career in politics. During this time, he served as Sergeant at Arms in the State Senate, and held the posts of County Assessor, Sheriff, and member of the Board of Levee Commissioners of the Mississippi River[110].

---

[106] https://www.nps.gov/places/blanche-kelso-bruce-house.htm
[107] https://www.nps.gov/places/blanche-kelso-bruce-house.htm
[108] https://www.historycentral.com/Bio/rec/BlancheBruce.html
[109] https://history.house.gov/People/Detail/10029
[110] https://www.britannica.com/biography/Blanche-K-Bruce

1874: After the Civil War, Bruce was the first formerly enslaved person to serve a full term in the U.S. Senate, and the first to preside over the Senate[111].

1875 - 1881: Bruce served in the 44th (1875–1877), 45th (1877–1879), and 46th (1879–1881) Congresses[112]. In 1878, he married socialite Josephine Beale Wilson; Reconstruction ended by that year. Due to increasing violence and attacks on the voting rights of African Americans in the Southern states, he did not run for the Senate in1880.

1880: He was the Presiding Officer over the Republican National Convention.

1881: Bruce was appointed Registrar of the US Treasury under President Garfield.

1889: He was Recorder of Deeds under President Harrison.

1883: Bruce was awarded an Honorary LL.D from Howard University and joined their Board of Trustees.

1897: He returned to the Treasury.

1898: Blanche Kelso Bruce died from Diabetes on March 17 in Washington, DC, and is buried in the Woodland Cemetery, Benning, District of Columbia, Washington, DC.

---

[111] https://www.rbhayes.org/collection-items/miscellaneous-manuscripts/bruce-blanche-kelso/

[112] https://history.house.gov/People/Detail/10029

[***NOTE:*** Blanche Kelso Bruce worked tirelessly advocating for the rights of Black Americans. Always pressing, he introduced a bill to provide government land in the West to aid poverty stricken Black farmers in Kansas. The bill died in Committee. He fought against the Chinese Exclusion Act, and advocated for fair treatment of Native Americans. His proposals usually died in discussion but he never wavered in his fight for social justice for his people and for other marginalized ethnic groups in America.

Bruce's life was politics. Sadly, he was never close to Black Americans who didn't believe he had their best interests at heart. Additionally, his constant protests and appeals began to distance him from White senators.]

JOSEPHINE ST. PIERRE RUFFIN [1842 – 1924]

Activist, Community Leader, Journalist, National Organizer, Publisher, Suffragist

Source: Bridgewater State University. Painted by T.A. Charron

1842: Josephine St. Pierre Ruffin was born in Beacon Hill, Massachusetts (MA), on August 31 to Elizabeth "Eliza" Matilda St. Pierre (formerly "Menhenick" from Cornwall England) and John St. Pierre, of French and African descent, from Martinique. She was raised in an activist, abolitionist environment and was educated in private schools. Her father was a successful businessman and founder of Boston Zion Church; Josephine enjoyed a life of ease.

1858: At age 16, she married George Ruffin, the first Black American graduate of Harvard Law School. She and her husband went to England due to the violence that preceded the passage of the Dred Scott *vs.* Sanford Supreme Court decision, which, in 1857, held that free or enslaved people of African descent were not U.S. citizens, had no rights under the U.S. Constitution, and slavery was legal[113]. The couple eventually returned home to America.

1861 - 1865: During the Civil War period Josephine and her husband helped to recruit Black men to fight in the
the 54th and 55th Massachusetts regiments on the Union side.

1869: She was a founding member of the American Woman Suffrage Association (AWSA), formed with Julia Howe and Lucy Stone, both White women. Julia Ward Howe was the author of "The Battle Hymn of the Republic."

1886: Josephine was widowed and left financially well off.

1890: After her husband's death, Ruffin launched the country's first newspaper for Black women, *The Woman's Era,* serving as its editor for seven years. The dual mission of the publication was to address the plight of Southern Blacks and provide members with opportunities for self-improvement[114].

---

[113] https://supreme.justia.com/cases/federal/us/60/393/

c. 1892 - 1894: Inspired by the newspaper's success, St. Pierre Ruffin founded the first Black women's philanthropic civic organization in Boston, *The Woman's Era Club*, which focused on charitable works. St. Pierre Ruffin remained its president until 1903. White women were also admitted as members to the club.

1895: St. Pierre Ruffin convened a conference of representatives of other national women's groups and the National Federation of Afro-American Women (NFAAW) was formed as a result of the conference. The mission of the NFAAW was to counter the negative image of Black women promoted by contemporaneous White publishers by demonstrating the existence of a large number of educated, cultured African-American women who were making meaningful contributions to society.

1896: The NFAAW merged with the Colored Women's League of Washington to become the National Association of Colored Women (NACW), and St. Pierre Ruffin was its first vice-president.

1910: She helped establish the first chapter of the National Association for the Advancement of Colored People in Massachusetts.

1920: She co-founded the League of Women for Community Service with her daughter, Florida Ruffin Widley, and purchased

---

[114] https://www.nps.gov/people/josephine-st-pierre-ruffin.htm

558 Massachusetts Avenue, Boston, MA, for its headquarters, where it remains in operation today.

1924: Josephine St. Pierre Ruffin died on March 13 and is buried in the Mount Auburn Cemetery, Middlesex County, in Cambridge, MA. She rests alongside her husband and other notable activists of her era.

[***NOTE:*** Josephine St. Pierre Ruffin dedicated her life to politics and the advancement of Black and other disadvantaged people in the U.S. She famously questioned the government's commitment to spend millions on war, but not a penny to stop the unprovoked lynchings and murder of Black Americans. Her lists of achievements are long and lasting—even into the 21st-century.

Not only was she a trailblazer in fighting for the rights and suffrage of all women, but Josephine's husband, George Ruffin was a trailblazer, too; he was the first Black man elected to the Boston City Council and was Boston's first African American municipal judge[115].]

---

[115] https://www.britannica.com/biography/Josephine-St-Pierre-Ruffin

BOSE IKARD
[1843 –1928]

Cowboy

Bose Ikard
Source: Public Domain

1843: Born into slavery in Summerville, Noxubee County, Mississippi, Bose Ikard acquired the complete range of cowboy skills, such as riding, roping, and fighting Indians on the cattle ranch where he lived.

1865: The Civil War ended. At the end of the Civil War he gained his freedom.

1866: He was hired as a trail driver for Oliver Loving.

1867: Charles Goodnight took over when Loving was killed and retained Ikard as a trail driver.

1869: Ikard bought land in Texas and raised a family there. He and Goodnight's relationship blossomed into a close friendship. Goodnight visited the Ikards often, bringing gifts of money.

1929: Bose Ikard died on January 4, in Weatherford, Texas (TX) and is buried in the Weatherford City Greenwood Cemetery, Park Country, USA.

[***NOTE***: Goodnight bought a headstone for Ikard's grave; on it was inscribed:

> "Served me 4 years on the Goodnight-Loving Trail. Never shirked a duty nor disobeyed an order. Rode with me in many stampedes. Participated in 3 engagements with Comanches. Splendid behavior—C. Goodnight."]

EMANUEL STANCE [1847? –1887]

Buffalo Soldier, National Hero

Emanuel Stance
Source: Public Domain

1847 or 1848: Emanuel Stance was born in East Carroll Parish, Louisiana, most likely to enslaved parents for, in the military records, he was described as a farmer[116]; the term used by the U.S. Army as a euphemism for "former slave". Army records show that he was literate, which hastened his upward mobility to the rank of Sergeant.

[116] According to Blackpast.org, "farmer" was a euphemism for "former slave", used by the U.S. Army.

1866: Stance enlisted in the army with the Troop F, African American 9th United States Calvary Regiment and served on the Western frontier for most of his active duty career[117].

1870: On July 24, 1870, Stance received the Congressional Medal of Honor, the country's highest award. The Medal of Honor was established during the civil war, for "unquestioned valor". On May 20, during the Battle of Kickapoo Springs, Stance had led a patrol to retrieve two children captured by the Kickapoo tribe[118]. It was a brutal two-day skirmish. Both children were rescued, as well as 15 horses captured from the Indians. Stance accomplished this feat with no loss of any soldiers. Emanuel Stance was the first Black officer to receive the Congressional Medal of Honor after the Civil War.

1887: Stance was murdered on Dec 25, supposedly by his own soldiers who rebelled against his harsh treatment toward them. He is buried at Fort McPherson National Cemetery, Maxwell in Lincoln County, Nebraska, U.S.A.

[***NOTE:*** The Black American soldiers of the 9th were responsible for controlling the Native American Plains Indians; reining in cattle rustlers; and protecting settlers, stagecoaches, and trains from Indian raids and bandits[119]. According to folklore, they became known as "Buffalo Soldiers", a name

---

[117] https://www.cem.va.gov

[118] https://www.thc.texas.gov/historic-sites/fort-mckavett/history/kickapoo-springs-skirmish

[119] https://www.history.com/topics/westward-expansion/buffalo-soldiers

bestowed on them by the Native Americans, for their bravery and the thick, curly hair on their heads, which reminded the Indians of the buffalo's fur.

At five feet tall, Stance was an interesting personality. He was intelligent, courageous, and also quick-tempered. He was reputed to be an extremely harsh disciplinarian, hated by his men, but respected by his commanders as an outstanding leader. During his 21 years in the Army he was jailed for drunkenness and abusive behavior, and repeatedly disciplined to the point of almost being court-martialed; however, he was also promoted repeatedly.]

SARAH E. GOODE [1855 –1905]

Inventor, Patent-holder, Entrepreneur

Sarah E. Goode
Source: Public Domain

1850 or 1855: Sarah Elisabeth Jacobs was born enslaved in Toledo, Lucas County, Ohio (OH), and gained freedom at the end of the Civil War. Jacobs came from a family of carpenters and was skilled in carpentry herself.

1870: After the Civil War Sarah's family moved to Chicago where she met and married Archibald Goode, a carpenter[120]. They opened a furniture store where they sold the furniture she designed for working-class people.[121]. She specialized in

[120] https://catalog.archives.gov/id/10601957

designing and creating efficient, multi-purpose furniture pieces for small spaces. She recognized that her customers had not only limited living space but also limited funds. With a desire to meet her customer's needs, she designed what she called a "Folding Cabinet Bed". The weight of Goode's folding bed was distributed in such a way that it could be opened and closed almost effortlessly. The bed was stable on each side, so it remained immobile during folding. When unfolded for use, there were supplementary supports to the center of the bed. This multifunctional bed could be folded into a roll-top desk, which included spaces for paper and supplies.

---

[121] https://drloihjournal.blogspot.com/2019/03/chicagoan-sarah-elisabeth-goode-was-first-negro-to-receive-a-US-patent.html

1885: On July 4, Goode received the first patent awarded to a Black American woman from the US Patent and Trademark Office that was signed in the recipient's own handwriting. The patent was for the folding cabinet bed, a single-bed precursor to the Murphy bed[122]. There is no information about Goode's life after her receipt of the patent.

1905: Sarah Goode died in Chicago, Cook County, Illinois and is buried in the Graceland Cemetery, Cook County, Chicago, IL.

[***NOTE:*** Judy W. Reed was the first known African American woman to receive a patent (September 23, 1884) for her dough-kneader[123]. However, Reed's patent was signed with her mark, an "x", and not her signature.]

---

122 https://www.lib.uchicago.edu/about/news/women-who-made-legal-history-sarah-e-goode/
123 https://www.ipwatchdog.com

OLIVER LEWIS
[1856 –1924]

Jockey

Oliver Lewis
Source: Public Domain

1856: Lewis was born free in Fayette County, Kentucky to Goodson and Eleanor Lewis[124].

1875: On May 17, 1875, Oliver Lewis, a 19 year old jockey, rode a horse named *Aristides* to victory on the first day of the opening of the Louisville Jockey Club (later renamed Churchill

[124] https://biography.jrank.org/pages/2969/Lewis-Oliver.html

Downs). Of the 15 jockeys to ride in the race, 13 were Black men; only two of the riders were Whites. According to the Smithsonian Magazine,

> "Among the first 28 derby winners, 15 were black. African-American jockeys excelled in the sport in the late 1800s. But by 1921, they had disappeared from the Kentucky track and would not return until Marlon St. Julien rode in the 2000 race[125]."

Bigotry against Blacks fueled the exclusion of Blacks as jockeys in the derby. Oliver rode 3 more horses to victory at the club and then stopped riding. He became a successful bookie at the track, which was legal at the time.

1924: Oliver Lewis died and was interred at the African Cemetery No. 2, Lexington, KY, which is also known as The Cemetery of the Union Benevolent Society No. 2.

[***NOTE:*** Very little is known about the early life of Oliver Lewis; however, he had two siblings, Isaac E. Lewis and George Garrett Lewis. Lewis was a husband and father of six children.

Black jockeys were the majority riders in the late 1800s. Black riders disappeared from the racing circuit until 2000.]

---

[125] https://www.smithsonianmag.com/history/the-kentucky-derbys-forgotten-jockeys-128781428/

HENRY OSSIAN FLIPPER
[1856 –1940]

West Point Cadet, Author

Henry Ossian Flipper
Source: Public Domain

1856: On March 21, Flipper was born a slave near Thomasville, Georgia, to parents Festus and Isabella Flipper. Henry was the oldest of their five sons.

c. 1865: Attended the American Missionary Association School in Georgia after the Civil War ended. His primary education was through the American Missionary Association.

1873: Flipper was appointed to the US Military Academy at West Point.

1877: He graduated and was commissioned as a Second Lieutenant, becoming the first African American to graduate from the Academy.

1878: Flipper was assigned to the 10th Cavalry and served on frontier duty in various installations in the Southwest, including Fort Sill, Oklahoma, until 1880. His duties included "scouting, as well as serving as post engineer surveyor and construction supervisor, post adjutant, acting assistant and post quartermaster, and commissary officer." (history.army.mil)[126] Black soldiers were known as Buffalo Soldiers, a name bestowed upon them by the Native American Indians out of respect for their prowess and bravery as fighters, and due to their hair, which resembled buffalo fur. Flipper wrote of his experiences at West Point in an autobiography entitled *The Colored Cadet at West Point.*

1879: He was the first Black officer to lead the Buffalo Soldiers. Under Captain Nicholas Nolan, Flipper led the Black soldiers into battle in New Mexico.

1881: At Fort Davis, he was framed by White officers and his Commanding Officer falsely accused him of embezzling $2000[127],

---

[126]https://history.army.mil/html/topics/afam/flipper.html
[127]According to the online CPI inflation calculator, $2,000.00 in 1882 was equivalent in purchasing power to about $54,233.14 in 2021, an increase of $52,233.14 over 139 years.

which he denied. Additionally, he was accused of conduct unbecoming an officer and a gentleman; subsequently, he was court-martialed on both charges. Although Flipper was acquitted of the embezzlement charges, but declared guilty of *Conduct Unbecoming an Officer and a Gentleman.*

1882: Flipper was dishonorably discharged from the Army after being convicted of the second charge.

1901 - 1912: His engineering skills gained him employment as a surveyor, a civil mining engineer, and a translator. As he was fluent in Spanish, he translated texts on Mexican tax laws, mining, and land laws[128].

1916: Flipper wrote his memoirs, which were published posthumously in 1963.

1921: He was an assistant to a US Senator in Washington DC.

1923: He worked as an engineer with a Venezuelan petroleum company; there, he translated that country's *Law on Hydrocarbons and Other Combustible Minerals.*

1931: He retired to the state of Georgia, where he lived with his brother.

---

[128] https://www.georgiaencyclopedia.org/articles/government-politics/henry-o-flipper-1856-1940/

1940: Henry O. Flipper died on April 26, 1940, aged 84. He was buried at Flipper Cemetery Thomasville, Thomas County, Georgia, USA.[129]

[***NOTE:*** His memoirs were first published posthumously in 1963 under the title *Negro Frontiersman: the Western Memoirs of Henry O. Flipper*. He fought the dishonorable conduct charges brought against him until his death.]

1976: He was granted a posthumous honorable discharge by President Jimmy Carter.

1999: President Bill Clinton granted a full presidential pardon to Flipper, posthumously.

---

[129] https://www.findagrave.com/memorial/19549/henry-ossian-flipper

PAULINE HOPKINS
[1859 –1930]

Author, Journalist, Editor

Pauline Hopkins
Source: Public Domain

1859: Pauline Elizabeth Hopkins was born free in Portland, ME, to Northrup Hopkins, a Civil War veteran and Sarah A. Hopkins, a former resident of Massachusetts (MA). Hopkins went to public school in Boston, MA. She became a successful author, using her mother's last name, "Allen", as her pen name. Hopkins was a well-known “colored soprano” at the end of the Reconstruction era.

1877: She performed in the lead role in Black theater.

1879: Hopkins produced the first colored musical drama, “Peculiar Sam”, a musical depicting slavery through the eyes of the enslaved. Hopkins’s Colored Troubadours traveled nationally performing in musical dramas. She was a contemporary of Booker T. Washington but disdained what she considered his “compromise” stance on racial equality issues of the day[130].

1880: She wrote her first play at 21 years of age.

1894: Washington invited her to become his stenographer; she declined.

1895: She became a stenographer for the Bureau of Statistic Massachusetts-Decennial Census.

1900: Hopkins’s first novel, *Contending Forces*, was published. It included accounts of the lynchings and cruel treatment of Black inmates. She was active in giving lectures and doing readings around the current events of the times

---

[130] In a speech that was subsequently labeled the “Atlanta Compromise”, Washington proposed that African Americans should “not agitate for social and political equality in return for the opportunity to acquire vocational training and participate in the economic development of the New South. He believed that through hard work and hard-earned respect, African Americans would gain the esteem of white society and eventually full citizenship.” https://blogs.loc.gov/teachers/2011/07/booker-t-washington-and-the-atlanta-compromise/

1901 - 1903: In 1901 Hopkins became a founding member of the Boston Literary and Historical Association. As editor of the Colored American Magazine, Hopkins had a platform for topics important in the Black intellectual community. Hopkins herself was outspoken and proactive in social justice causes. After publication of *Contending Forces,* she authored three novels in serial form, cleverly intertwining romance and adventure to showcase race issues; these were *Hagar's Daughter: A Story of Southern Caste Prejudice*, *Winona: A Tale of Negro Life in the South and Southwest,* and *Of One Blood; Or, The Hidden Self*[131]. Of her three novels, *Hagar's Daughter* has been revived.

1904: Booker T. Washington bought the Colored American Magazine, eventually removing Hopkins from her position. She took a position as editor of the New Era magazine.

1930: On August 13, Pauline Hopkins perished from burns in an oil stove fire in Boston, Suffolk County; MA. She was interred at the Cambridge Cemetery, Cambridge, Middlesex County, MA.

---

[131] https://www.paulinehopkinssociety.org/biography/

IDA B. WELLS
[1862 – 1931]

Journalist, Activist, Leader, Educator, Author

Ida B. Wells
Source: Public Domain

1862: On July 16, Ida Bell Wells was born into slavery in Holly Springs, Mississippi. She was the oldest daughter of James and Lizzie Wells. The entire family was freed by the Emancipation Proclamation of September 22 of that year. Lizzie's parents became politically active in the Republican Party. Her father helped establish Shaw University, a school for freed slaves.

1878: Wells attended Rust College, a freedman's school[132], in Holly Springs until 1878 when her parents and one of her six siblings died in the yellow fever epidemic[133].

1882: Wells moved to Memphis, Tennessee (TN).

1883 – 1891: Wells taught in the Memphis, Tennessee public schools.

1884: She brought suit against the Chesapeake and Ohio Rail Road Company. Having bought a first class ticket on the Nashville to Memphis train, she was forcibly removed from her seat. During the altercation, she bit one of the crew members. Wells won in the circuit court and was awarded $500. The Tennessee Supreme Court later overturned her victory. She was required to return $200.

1888: *The Free Speech and Headlight*, a local Black-owned newspaper edited by Wells, gave her a forum to speak out against racial inequity. Wells bought a share of the newspaper[134]. Through the newspaper Wells launched an anti-lynching campaign, which documented atrocities against Black men and women. These lynchings were generally based on lies and fabrications.

---

[132] https://www.britannica.com/biography/Ida-B-Wells-Barnett#ref138160
[133] https://awpc.cattcenter.iastate.edu/directory/ida-b-wells/
[134] https://bit.ly/3DNJlHA

1891: Wells was fired from her teaching job for exposing the unequal provisions distributed between Black and White schools.

1892: Wells published a story on a lynching event entitled "People's Grocery Lynching". According to reports, a White grocer, Will Barrett, jealous over the success of three Black owners of *The People's Grocery,* initiated a complaint against the store's owners in which he accused them of being a public nuisance. The Black storeowners were arrested and eventually lynched by a mob of White men. The incident became known as *The Curve Riots*. Due to her reporting of the event, the newspaper gained national attention. From interviews, news articles and pictures, Wells formed a picture of the reality and frequency of lynchings of Black people in the south.

1892: Wells published "Southern Horrors and Mob rule in New Orleans".

1892 - 1893: Wells published "Southern Horrors: Lynch Law in all its Phases".

Whites in Memphis were so incensed by her words they wrecked her office, beat her employee, and threatened to murder her if she returned.

1894: Wells traveled to England. While in Europe, she established the British Anti-Lynching Society.

1895: She published the "Red Record", a 100 page booklet, which was the first written account—with statistics—on the history of the lynching of Blacks.

Ida Wells moved to Chicago and married Ferdinand L. Barnett. They travelled widely, including to England, speaking on the evils of lynching. Wells upbraided the Suffrage movement for ignoring the issue of lynching. The movement's leadership retaliated by excluding and denouncing her. Wells was present when the NAACP was started but is not listed as a founder. It may be because she wanted the organization to engage in more activism and this was a fledgling organization perhaps not yet ready for extreme moves. In Chicago, Wells-Barnett wrote full-time for the Daily Inter Ocean and took over control of the city's oldest Black paper, *The Chicago Conservator.*

1898: Wells-Barnett met with President McKinley in Washington, DC to discuss making lynching illegal.

1908: She separated from the NAACP over their moderate reaction to violent attacks on Blacks in Springfield, Illinois (Il).

1910: She established the Negro Fellowship League to help elevate the possibilities for Black men. The league operated until1923.

1913: She formed the first Kindergarten for Black children and also formed the Alpha Suffrage Club, which was designed to focus on candidates sympathetic to "the Black situation". The club was influential in the passing of the Illinois Equal Suffrage Act, June, 1913. The Alpha clubs are still operating.

1931: On March 26, Ida B. Wells-Barnett died in Chicago, IL, and is interred in the Oak Woods Cemetery, Chicago, Cook County, Illinois, and U.S.A.[135]

[***NOTE***: In 1974 The Ida B. Wells House in Chicago, her private residence, was added to the National Historic Landmark list. In 2020, Wells was awarded, posthumously, a Pulitzer Prize for great journalism under extreme danger in exposing the truth about the evil, hateful, and illegal acts of violence perpetrated on Black American men by White men.

She published some of her articles under the byname: "Lola"]

---

135 https://www.findagrave.com/memorial/7862236/ida-bell-wells

SCOTT JOPLIN
[c. 1867 – 1917]

Composer, Pianist a.k.a. "King of Ragtime"

Scott Joplin
Source: Public Domain

1867 or 1868: Joplin was probably born in the northeast part of Texas. The US Census records his presence there in July 1870, when he was two years old[136]. His family moved to Texarkana, a newly established town straddling the Texas-Arkansas border. Supposedly, Joplin taught himself piano in the home of the White family for whom his mother worked.

---

[136] https://www.scottjoplin.org/joplin-biography.html

1880's(?): Julian Weiss, a local music teacher, recognized Joplin's potential. Professor Weiss gave Joplin free lessons.

In his 20s, Joplin traveled around the South, playing anywhere he could.

1893: He formed a band and performed at the Chicago World's Fair where he introduced "ragtime", a syncopated off-standard rhythm piano style.

1899: Joplin published *Maple Leaf Rag*, perhaps his most famous piece, which sold over one million paper copies.

1903: He composed an Opera, *Guest of Honor*, which failed due to corrupt managing and poor showings. It never reached full production. The score has been lost.

1904: Married Freddie Alexander, who died 10 weeks after the marriage.

1908: Joplin self-published *School of Ragtime*.

1911: He Composed *Treemonisha*, his second opera, which may have been inspired with events in his life and his philosophy about African American advancement in America[137]. This opera suffered a similar fate as his first opera; however, this work was not lost and was revived in 1972. Joplin was a prolific composer,

---

[137]https://web.archive.org/web/20050526170546/http://www.cbmr.org/pubs/132/ragtime132.htm

but by the time *Treemonisha* was published, Ragtime was fading in popularity.

1916: Joplin was hospitalized with syphilis.

1917: Scott Joplin succumbed to his disease and is buried at Saint Michel's Cemetery, New Your, New York County, Manhattan, NY.

[***NOTE:*** In 1973, the very popular and successful movie, *The Sting*, saw a revival in Ragtime music. *The Entertainer*, a musical piece composed by Scott Joplin, was the background sound track for that movie.

1976: Joplin was awarded the Pulitzer Prize 60 years after he died.]

MADAME C. J. WALKER [1867–1919]

Entrepreneur, Millionaire, Philanthropist, Political and Social Activist

Madam C. J. Walker
Source: Public Domain

1867: Sarah Breedlove (a.k.a. Madame C.J. Walker) was born on a cotton plantation near Delta, Louisiana on December 23[138], after the Emancipation Proclamation of January 1, 1863, and two years and eight months after the U.S. Civil War effectively ended on April 9, 1865. Her parents, Owen and Minerva Breedlove, formerly enslaved, were sharecroppers at the time of her birth. Of their six children, Sarah was the first child born free[139].

[138] Note: Some accounts place the sharecropping farm in Delta, Louisiana.

1873 - 1874: She was orphaned at age seven and sent to live with her married sister Louvinia and her husband, Jesse Powell. Louvinia's husband, reputedly, was an abusive man[140].

1877: The three moved to Vicksburg, Mississippi, where Sarah worked picking cotton and doing housework for Whites[141].

1881: At aged 14, she married Moses McWilliams—perhaps to escape her abusive brother-in-law.

1885: At the age of 18, Sarah gave birth to a daughter, Lelia, whose name was changed later to "A'Lelia".

1887: Sarah was widowed at age 20, when A'Lelia was 2 years old. She and A'Lelia moved to St. Louis where she worked as a laundress and attended night school.

1894: At the age of 27 Sarah married John Davis, and divorced him around 1903.

1906: She married Charles J. Walker, her third husband, an advertising salesman.

1907: By this time, Madam C.J. Walker had developed her own brand of products for African/Black American hair type. Her husband helped her develop and brand her fledgling hair products business under the name "The Madam C.J. Walker

---

[139] https://www.history.com/topics/black-history/madame-c-j-walker
[140] Note: Some accounts state Sarah Breedlove was orphaned at age 6.
[141] https://www.biography.com/inventor/madam-cj-walker

Company". With her husband's help they developed a mail order business.

1907: She traveled through the south marketing her products and demonstrating the "Walker Method" of hair care. She touted the African origins of the materials used in her products.

1908: Walker built a factory in Pittsburg, Pennsylvania, and a beauty school. At the school, she trained women to not only sell products, but also how to enhance and improve themselves as individuals through learning proper body care and grooming. She taught them how to dress professionally, and how to comport themselves with poise. These women would be "Walker's Agents". Her agents sold the product line by promoting themselves as women of style and grace. In her life, she trained and groomed up to 40,000 Black women. She told Black women they mattered. She used Black newspapers to advertise her products and used her image to show the before and after effectiveness of her hair growing products.

1910: Walker incorporated the business; it became The Walker Manufacturing Company, Inc.; she was the only shareholder. Using $10,000 of her own money, she expanded her product line to include shampoos, creams, diets, and hot combs (which was not her invention).

1912: Sarah Walker divorced her husband but retained the brand name "Madam C.J. Walker Company, Inc." .

1917: She organized the National Negro Cosmetics Manufacturer's Association[142]. The convention's first meeting focused solely on business-building for Blacks.

1915: She created "Hints to Agents", a manual to aid her agents in the field.

1916: Walker built a mansion in New York, which she named *Villa Lewaro.*

1919: On May 25, 51 years of age, Madame C.J. Walker died of hypertension at Villa Lewaro [143]. She was buried at Woodlawn Cemetery in the Bronx, New York.

[***NOTE:*** During the 1890s, Sarah suffered serious hair loss due to a combination of poor living conditions and stress. After trying various products to no avail, Sarah began using—with great success—a line of Black hair products developed by a Black entrepreneur, Annie Turnbo Malone. She eventually became a commissioned sales agent for Turnbo, and moved to Denver, Colorado in 1905. No doubt, Sarah learned the fundamentals of the hair care business from Turnbo.

It is worth noting that Black business owners were few; race discrimination and start-up costs made going into business almost impossible. However, for Black women, hairdressing was a more easily affordable venture. Reportedly, Sarah had a dream

[142] https://images.indianahistory.org/digital/collection/m0399/id/6375
[143] https://www.biography.com/inventor/madam-cj-walker

in which a Black man told her what she would need to develop a line of hair products for Black women, and where to purchase products for the line: *Africa.* After her 'dream', she ordered items from Africa and applied them to her scalp. Her hair grew rapidly. At one point, Walker worked for a pharmacist and may have picked up some knowledge of chemicals during the course of her employment. The Madam C.J. Walker brand is still being sold today[144].]

---

[144] https://www.townandcountrymag.com/style/beauty-products/a31941847/madam-cj-walker-hair-products-sephora-shop/

WILLIAM M. "BILL" PICKETT [1870 –1932]

Cowboy; Creator of the Bulldog (Steer-wrestling) Technique

William M. "Bill" Pickett
Source: Public Domain

c. 1870: William Pickett, one of 13 children, was born in Williamson County, Texas (TX) to Thomas Jefferson Pickett and Mary "Janie" Pickett, both formerly enslaved. The family was of mixed ancestry (African, White, and Cherokee)[145]. Pickett had a fifth-grade education before becoming a ranch hand. Called

[145] https://americacomesalive.com/bill-pickett-ca-1870-1932-african-american-cowboy/

"Will" as a youngster, he learned branding and rope handling, eventually developing his own roping technique.

c. 1880s: Pickett invented a technique called bulldogging which is described as "grasping it by the horns, twisting its neck, biting its nose or its upper lip, and making it fall on its side"[146]; today, the maneuver is also known as "steer-wrestling"[147]. Throughout the 1880s, he worked at different ranches.

1880s: Picket and his brothers launched their own horse-breaking services, the Pickett Brothers Bronco Busters and Rough Riders Association, in Taylor, TX. They claimed they could break any horse and catch and tame stray cattle.

1888: Pickett entered his first rodeo in Taylor, TX; throughout his rodeo career, he had to register as an Indian to compete against White men as Black cowboys were banned from participation in the sport.

1890: He married Maggie Turner, a former slave; she was the daughter of a White former slave owner[148].

1900s: Pickett became a popular rodeo attraction, touring the West and demonstrating his bulldogging technique, which is still one of rodeo's most important events today.

---

146 https://www.okhistory.org/publications/enc/entry.php?entry=PI003
147 https://www.hmdb.org/m.asp?m=52777
148 https://www.legendsofamerica.com/bill-pickett/

1904 or 1905: He joined the Millers Brothers 101 show and performed with some famous cowboys, one of whom was Tom Mix.

1908: He and his horse suffered were injured while performing in a rodeo.

1920s: Pickett retired from the shows but still gave exhibitions and was featured in a few western movies. He went back to the Miller ranch.

1932: Bill Pickett died on April 2, in Marland, Noble County, Oklahoma, kicked in the head by a horse. He is buried at White Eagle Monument, Marland, Noble County, Oklahoma.

[***NOTE:*** In Pickett's eulogy, Miller wrote that Pickett was the "greatest sweat and dirt cowhand that ever lived-bar none.[149]"]

---

[149] https://nationalcowboymuseum.org/

About Miriam Y. McCarthy

Miriam Y. McCarthy holds a Bachelor of Science degree in education from Chicago State University, and graduate hours from the University of New Hampshire. She taught history in the Chicago public school system.

Her interests and pursuits signal an eclectic and entrepreneurial nature. In the past, she launched and owned various types of retail businesses, and was also an antique dealer for many years.

After retiring, her interest has turned to writing. A prolific writer of poetry, this book is her first venture into historical nonfiction literature.

Miriam looks forward to sharing her insights about the Black American experience with the world.

DATE DUE

Made in the USA
Middletown, DE
06 March 2022

62121982R00070